Understanding the Consumer Price Index: Answers to Some Questions

U.S. Department of Labor
Bureau of Labor Statistics
August 2004 (Revised)

QUESTIONS & ANSWERS

Introduction

The continually growing number of uses and users of the Consumer Price Index (CPI) has generated an increasing number of questions about the CPI. Although the Bureau of Labor Statistics (BLS; the Bureau) has provided extensive material to the public describing the CPI, much of this material has been quite technical. The Bureau has developed this pamphlet, therefore, to

- answer frequently asked questions about the CPI and

- help users of the CPI to better understand and use it.

Information in this publication will be made available to sensory-impaired individuals upon request. Voice phone: (202) 691-5200; Federal Relay Service: 1-800-877-8339.

QUESTIONS & ANSWERS

Contents

What is the CPI?

1

The Consumer Price Index (CPI) is a measure of the average change over time in the prices paid by urban consumers for a market basket of consumer goods and services.

How is the CPI used?

2

The CPI affects nearly all Americans, because of the many ways in which it is used. Following are three major uses:

1. *As an economic indicator.* The CPI is the most widely used measure of inflation and is sometimes viewed as an indicator of the effectiveness of government economic policy. It provides information about price changes in the Nation's economy to government, business, labor, and private citizens and is used by them as a guide to making economic decisions. In addition, the President, Congress, and the Federal Reserve Board use trends in the CPI to aid in formulating fiscal and monetary policies.

2. *As a deflator of other economic series.* The CPI and its components are used to adjust other economic series for price changes and to translate these series into inflation-free dollars. Examples of series adjusted by the CPI include retail sales, hourly and weekly earnings, and components of the National Income and Product Accounts.

   An interesting example is to use the CPI as a deflator of the value of the consumer's dollar to find its purchasing power. The purchasing power of the consumer's dollar measures the change in the value to the consumer of the goods and services that a dollar will buy at different dates. In other words, as prices increase, the purchasing power of the consumer's dollar declines.

3. *As a means of adjusting dollar values.* The CPI is often used to adjust consumers' income payments (for example, Social Security), to adjust income eligibility levels for government assistance, and to automatically provide cost-of-living wage adjustments to millions of American workers.

As a result of statutory action, the CPI affects the income of almost 80 million persons: 51.6 million Social Security beneficiaries, about 21.3 million Food Stamp recipients, and about 4.6 million military and Federal Civil Service retirees and survivors. Changes in the CPI also affect the cost of lunches for 28.4 million children who eat lunch at school, while collective bargaining agreements that tie wages to the CPI cover almost 2 million workers.

Another example of how dollar values may be adjusted is the use of the CPI to adjust the Federal income tax structure. These adjustments prevent inflation-induced increases in tax rates, an effect called *bracket creep.*

Whose buying habits does the CPI reflect?

3

The CPI reflects spending patterns for each of two population groups: *All urban consumers* and *urban wage earners and clerical workers.* The all-urban consumer group represents about 87 percent of the total U.S. population. It is based on the expenditures of almost all residents of urban or metropolitan areas, including professionals, the self-employed, the poor, the unemployed, and retired persons, as well as urban wage earners and clerical workers. Not included in the CPI are the spending patterns of persons living in rural nonmetropolitan areas, farm families, persons in the Armed Forces, and those in institutions, such as prisons and mental hospitals. The price-change experience of the all-urban consumer group is measured by two indexes, namely, the traditional Consumer Price Index for All Urban Consumers (CPI-U) and the newer Chained Consumer Price Index for All Urban Consumers (C-CPI-U). (See answer to Question 4 for an explanation of the differences between the CPI-U and C-CPI-U.)

The Consumer Price Index for Urban Wage Earners and Clerical Workers (CPI-W) is based on the expenditures of households included in the CPI-U definition that also meet two requirements: More than one-half of the household's income must come from clerical or wage occupations, and at least one of the household's earners must have been employed for at least 37 weeks during the previous 12 months. The CPI-W's population represents about 32 percent of the total U.S. population and is a subset, or part, of the CPI-U's population.

Is the CPI a cost-of-living index?

4

The CPI frequently is called a cost-of-living index, but it differs in important ways from a complete cost-of-living measure. BLS has for some time used a cost-of-living framework in making practical decisions about questions that arise in constructing the CPI. A cost-of-living index is a conceptual measurement goal, however, not a straightforward alternative to the CPI. A cost-of-living index would measure changes over time in the amount that consumers need to spend to reach a certain *utility level* or *standard of living*. Both the CPI and a cost-of-living index would reflect changes in the prices of goods and services, such as food and clothing, that are directly purchased in the marketplace; but a complete cost-of-living index would go beyond this role to also take into account changes in other governmental or environmental factors that affect consumers' well-being. It is very difficult to determine the proper treatment of public goods, such as safety and education, and other broad concerns, such as health, water quality, and crime, that would constitute a complete cost-of-living framework.

Traditionally, the CPI was considered an upper bound on a cost-of-living index, in that the CPI did not reflect the changes in buying or consumption patterns that consumers would make to adjust to relative price changes. The ability to substitute means that the increase in the cost to consumers of maintaining their level of well-being tends to be somewhat less than the increase in the cost of the mix of goods and services they previously purchased.

Since January 1999, a geometric mean formula has been used to calculate most basic indexes within the CPI; in other words, the prices within most item categories (for example, apples) are averaged with the use of a geometric mean formula. This improvement moves the CPI somewhat closer to a cost-of-living measure, because the geometric mean formula allows for a modest amount of consumer substitution as relative prices within item categories change.

Because the geometric mean formula is used only to average prices within item categories, it does not account for consumer substitution taking place *between* item categories. For example, if the price of pork increases relative to the prices of other meats, shoppers might shift their purchases away from pork to beef, poultry, or fish. The traditional CPI formula did not reflect this type of consumer response to changing relative prices. In 2002, as a complement to the CPI-U and CPI-W, the Bureau produced a new index called the Chained CPI-U (C-CPI-U). The C-CPI-U was created to more closely approximate a cost-of-living index by reflecting substitution among item categories. It is unlikely, however, that the difficult problems of defining living standards and measuring changes in the cost of their attainment over time ever will be resolved completely.

It is important to note that local-area CPIs cannot be used to compare levels of living costs or prices across areas. (See answer to Question 18: "Can the CPIs for individual areas be used to compare living costs among areas?")

Does the CPI measure my experience with price change?

5

Not necessarily. It is important to understand that BLS bases the market baskets and pricing procedures for the U- and W-populations on the experience of the relevant *average* household, not of any specific family or individual. It is unlikely that your experience will correspond precisely with either the national indexes or the indexes for specific cities or regions.

For example, if you or your family spend a larger-than-average share of your budget on medical expenses, and medical care costs are increasing more rapidly than the cost of other items in the CPI market basket, your personal rate of inflation (or experience with price changes) may exceed the increase in the CPI. Conversely, if you heat your home with solar energy, and fuel prices are rising more rapidly than other items, you may experience less inflation than the general population does.

A national average reflects all the ups and downs of millions of individual price experiences. It seldom mirrors a particular consumer's experience.

How is the CPI market basket determined?

6

The CPI market basket is developed from detailed expenditure information provided by families and individuals on what they actually bought. For the current CPI, this information was collected from the Consumer Expenditure Survey over the 2 years 2001 and 2002. In each of these years, about 10,000 families from around the country provided information on their spending habits in a series of quarterly interviews. To collect information on frequently purchased items, such as food and personal care products, another 7,500 families in each of the 2 years kept diaries listing everything they bought during a 2-week period.

Altogether, more than 30,000 individuals and families provided expenditure information for use in determining the importance, or weight, of the over 200 item categories in the CPI index structure.

What goods and services does the CPI cover?

The CPI represents all goods and services purchased for consumption by the reference population (U or W). BLS has classified all expenditure items into more than 200 categories, arranged into eight major groups. Major groups and examples of categories in each are as follows:

- FOOD AND BEVERAGES (breakfast cereal, milk, coffee, chicken, wine, full-service meals, and snacks)

- HOUSING (rent of primary residence, owners' equivalent rent, fuel oil, bedroom furniture)

- APPAREL (men's shirts and sweaters, women's dresses, jewelry)

- TRANSPORTATION (new vehicles, airline fares, gasoline; motor vehicle insurance)

- MEDICAL CARE (prescription drugs and medical supplies, physicians' services, eyeglasses and eye care, hospital services)

- RECREATION (televisions, toys, pets, and pet products, sports equipment, admissions)

- EDUCATION AND COMMUNICATION (college tuition, postage, telephone services, computer software and accessories)

- OTHER GOODS AND SERVICES (tobacco and smoking products, haircuts and other personal services, funeral expenses)

Also included within these major groups are various government-charged user fees, such as water and sewerage charges, auto registration fees, and vehicle tolls. In addition, the CPI includes taxes (such as sales and excise taxes) that are directly associated with the prices of specific goods and services. However, the CPI excludes taxes (such as income and Social Security taxes) not directly associated with the purchase of consumer goods and services.

The CPI does not include investment items, such as stocks, bonds, real estate, and life insurance. (These items relate to savings and not to day-to-day consumption expenses.)

For each of the more than 200 item categories, using scientific statistical procedures, the Bureau has chosen samples of several hundred specific items within selected consumer-frequented business establishments to represent the thousands of varieties available in the marketplace. For example, in a given supermarket, the Bureau may choose a plastic bag of golden delicious apples, U.S. extra fancy grade, weighing 4.4 pounds, to represent the *apples* category.

How are CPI prices collected and reviewed? 8

Each month, BLS data collectors, called *economic assistants* visit or call thousands of retail stores, service establishments, rental units, and doctors' offices, all over the United States, to obtain price information on the prices of thousands of items used to track and measure price change in the CPI. These economic assistants record the prices of about 80,000 items each month, representing a scientifically selected sample of the prices paid by consumers for the goods and services purchased.

During each call or visit, the economic assistant collects price data on a specific good or service that was precisely defined during an earlier visit. If the selected item is available, the economic assistant records its price. If the selected item is no longer available, or if there have been changes in the quality or quantity (for example, eggs sold in packages of eight, when previously they had been sold by the dozen) of the good or service since the last time prices were collected, the economic assistant selects a new item or records the quality change in the current item.

The recorded information is sent to the national office of BLS, where commodity specialists who have detailed knowledge about the particular goods or services priced review the data. These specialists check the data for accuracy and consistency and make any necessary corrections or adjustments, which can range from an adjustment for a change in the size or quantity of a packaged item to more complex adjustments based upon statistical analysis of the value of an item's features or quality. Thus, the commodity specialists strive to prevent changes in the quality of items from affecting the CPI's measurement of price change.

How is the CPI calculated?

The CPI is a product of a series of interrelated samples. First, using data from the 1990 Census of Population, BLS selected the urban areas from which data on prices were collected and chose the housing units within each area that were eligible for use in the shelter component of the CPI. The Census of Population also provided data on the number of consumers represented by each area selected as a CPI price collection area. Next, another sample (of about 16,800 families each year) served as the basis for a Point-of-Purchase Survey that identified the places where households purchased various types of goods and services.

Data from the Consumer Expenditure Survey conducted in 2001 and 2002, involving a national sample of more than 30,000 families, provided detailed information on respondents' spending habits. This information enabled BLS to construct the CPI market basket of goods and services and to assign each item in the market basket a weight, or importance, based on total family expenditures. The final stage in the sampling process is the selection of the specific detailed item to be priced in each outlet. This is done in the field, using a method called *disaggregation*. For example, BLS economic assistants may be directed to price "fresh whole milk." Through the disaggregation process, the economic assistant selects the specific kind of fresh whole milk that will be priced in the outlet over time. By this process, each kind of whole milk is assigned a probability of selection, or weight, based on the amount the store sells. If, for example, Vitamin D, homogenized milk in half-gallon containers makes up 70 percent of the sales of whole milk, and the same milk in quart containers accounts for 10 percent of all whole-milk sales, then the half-gallon container will be 7 times as likely to be chosen as the quart container. After probabilities are assigned, one type, brand, and container size of milk is chosen by an objective selection process based on the theory of random sampling. The particular kind of milk that is selected by disaggregation will continue to be priced each month in the same outlet.

In sum, the price movement measurement (Question 8) is weighted by the importance of the item in the spending patterns of the appropriate population group. The combination of all these factors gives a weighted measurement of price change for all items in all outlets, in all areas priced for the CPI.

How are taxes treated in the CPI? 10

Certain taxes are included in the CPI, namely, taxes that are directly associated with the purchase of specific goods and services (such as sales and excise taxes). Government user fees are also included in the

CPI. For example, toll charges and parking fees are included in the transportation category, and an entry fee to a national park would be included as part of the admissions index. In addition, property taxes should be reflected indirectly in the BLS method of measuring the cost of the flow of services provided by housing shelter, which we called *owners' equivalent rent*, to the extent that these taxes influence rental values. Taxes not directly associated with specific purchases, such as income and Social Security taxes, are excluded, as are the government services paid for through those taxes.

For certain purposes, one might want to define price indexes to include, rather than exclude, income taxes. Such indexes would provide an answer to a question different from the one to which the present CPI is relevant and would be appropriate for different uses.

How do I read or interpret an index?

An index is a tool that simplifies the measurement of movements in a numerical series. Most of the specific CPI indexes have a 1982–84 reference base. That is, BLS sets the average index level (representing the average price level)—for the 36-month period covering the years 1982, 1983, and 1984—equal to 100. BLS then measures changes in relation to that figure. An index of 110, for example, means that there has been a 10-percent increase in price since the reference period; similarly an index of 90 means a 10-percent decrease. Movements of the index from one date to another can be expressed as changes in index points (simply, the difference between index levels), but it is more useful to express the movements as percent changes. This is because index points are affected by the level of the index in relation to its reference period, while percent changes are not.

In the table that follows, Item A increased by half as many index points as Item B between Year I and Year II. Yet, because of the different starting figures, both items had the same percent change; that is, prices advanced at the same rate. By contrast, Items B and C show the same change in index points, but the percent change is greater for Item C because of its lower starting value.

	Item A	Item B	Item C
Year I	112.5	225.0	110.0
Year II	121.5	243.0	128.0
Change in index points	9.0	18.0	18.0
Percent change	$9.0/112.5 \times 100 = 8.0$	$18.0/225.0 \times 100 = 8.0$	$18.0/110.0 \times 100 = 16.4$

Is the CPI the best measure of inflation?

12

Inflation has been defined as a process of continuously rising prices or, equivalently, of a continuously falling value of money.

Various indexes have been devised to measure different aspects of inflation. The CPI measures inflation as experienced by consumers in their day-to-day living expenses; the Producer Price Index (PPI) measures inflation at earlier stages of the production and marketing process; the Employment Cost Index (ECI) measures it in the labor market; the BLS International Price Program measures it for imports and exports; and the Gross Domestic Product Deflator (GDP Deflator) measures combine the experience with inflation of governments (Federal, State, and local), businesses, and consumers. Finally, there are specialized measures, such as measures of interest rates and measures of consumers' and business executives' expectations of inflation.

The "best" measure of inflation for a given application depends on the intended use of the data. The CPI is generally the best measure for adjusting payments to consumers when the intent is to allow consumers to purchase at today's prices, a market basket of goods and services equivalent to one that they could purchase in an earlier period. The CPI also is the best measure to use to translate retail sales and hourly or weekly earnings into real, or inflation-free, dollars.

Which index is the "official CPI" reported in the media?

Each month, BLS releases thousands of detailed CPI numbers to the media. However, the media usually focuses on the broadest, most comprehensive CPI: *The Consumer Price Index for All Urban Consumers (CPI-U) for the U.S. City Average for All Items, 1982–84=100*. These data are reported on either a seasonally adjusted or an unadjusted basis. Often, the media will report some, or all, of the following:

a. index level, not seasonally adjusted (for example, May 2001 = 177.7).

b. 12-month percent change, not seasonally adjusted (for example, May 2000 to May 2001= 3.6 percent).

c. 1-month percent change on a seasonally adjusted basis (for example, from April 2001 to May 2001 = 0.5 percent).

d. annual rate of percent change so far this year (for example, from December 2000 to May 2001, if the rate of increase over the first 5 months of the year continued for the full year, after the removal of seasonal influences, the rise would be 3.9 percent).

e. annual rate based on the latest seasonally adjusted 1-month change (for example, if the rate from April 2001 to May 2001 continued for a full 12 months, then the rise, compounded, would be 6.3 percent).

What index should I use for escalation?

The decision to employ an escalation mechanism,

as well as the choice of the most suitable index, is up to the user. When the terms of an escalation provision for use in a contract to adjust future payments are drafted, both legal and statistical questions can arise. While BLS cannot help in any matters relating to legal questions, it does provide basic technical and statistical assistance to users who are developing indexing procedures.

Following are some examples of technical or statistical guidelines from BLS:

• For escalation, BLS strongly recommends using indexes that are unadjusted for seasonal variation. (See the answer to Question 15 for a further explanation of seasonally adjusted indexes and the reasons BLS doesn't recommend seasonally adjusted indexes for use in escalation.)

• Also for escalation, BLS recommends using national or regional indexes, due to the volatility of local indexes. (See the answer to Question 16 for an explanation of this point.)

For those with further questions, BLS has prepared a detailed report, *Using the Consumer Price Index for Escalation.* This information also may be obtained on the CPI homepage at **http://www.bls.gov/cpi/** or by writing or calling the nearest BLS regional office listed in the answer to Question 22. You also may call the BLS national office at (202) 691-7000.

When should I use seasonally adjusted data? 15

By using seasonally adjusted data, economic analysts and the media find it easier to see the underlying trend in short-term price changes. It is often difficult to tell from raw (unadjusted) statistics whether developments between any 2 months reflect changing economic conditions or only normal seasonal patterns. Therefore, many economic series, including the CPI, are adjusted to remove the effect of seasonal influences—those which occur at the same time and in about the same magnitude every year. Among these influences are price movements resulting from changing climatic conditions, production cycles, changeovers of models, and holidays.

BLS annually reestimates the factors that are used to seasonally adjust CPI data, and seasonally adjusted indexes that have been published earlier are subject to revision for up to 5 years after their original release. Therefore, unadjusted data are more appropriate for escalation purposes.

What area indexes are published and how often 16

Besides monthly publication of the national (or U.S. City Average) CPI-U, C-CPI-U, and CPI-W, indexes are published by area for the CPI-U and CPI-W. For the C-CPI-U, data for all items and 27 components are available at the national level only; for the CPI-U and CPI-W, 377 component series are published at the national level. Monthly CPI-U and CPI-W indexes are published for the four census regions: Northeast, Midwest (formerly North Central), South, and West. Monthly indexes also are published for urban areas classified by population size: All metropolitan areas over 1.5 million, metropolitan areas smaller than 1.5 million, and all nonmetropolitan urban areas. Indexes are available as well within each region, cross-classified by area population size. For the Northeast and West, however, indexes for nonmetropolitan areas are not available. BLS also publishes indexes for 27 local areas. These indexes are byproducts of the national CPI program. Each local index has a much smaller sample size than the national or regional indexes and is, therefore, subject to substantially more sampling and other measurement error. As a result, local area indexes are more volatile than the national or regional indexes, and BLS strongly urges users to consider adopting the national or regional CPIs for use in escalator clauses. Used with caution, local area CPI data can illustrate and explain the impact of local economic conditions on consumers' experience with price change. Local area data are available on the following schedule:

BLS publishes three major metropolitan areas monthly:

Chicago–Gary–Kenosha, IL–IN–WI
Los Angeles–Riverside–Orange County, CA
New York–Northern NJ–Long Island, NY–NJ–CT–PA

Data for the following additional 11 metropolitan areas are published every other month [on an odd (January, March, etc.) or even (February, April, etc.) month schedule] for the following areas:

Atlanta, GA	even	Miami–Fort Lauderdale, FL	even
Boston–Brockton–Nashua, MA–NH–ME–CT	odd	Philadelphia–Wilmington–Atlantic City, PA–NJ–DE–MD	even
Cleveland–Akron, OH	odd	San Franciso–Oakland-San Jose, CA	even
Dallas–Fort Worth, TX	odd	Seattle–Tacoma–Bremerton, WA	even
Detroit–Ann Arbor–Flint, MI	even	Washington–Baltimore, DC–MD–VA–WV	odd
Houston–Galveston–Brazoria, TX	even		

(*Note:* The designation *even* or *odd* refers to the month during which the area's price change is measured. Because of the time needed for processing, data are released 2 to 3 weeks into the following month.)

Data are published for another group of 13 metropolitan areas on a semiannual basis. These indexes, which refer to the arithmetic average for the 6-month periods from January through June and July and January, respectively, in August and February for the following areas:

Anchorage, AK	Phoenix–Mesa, AZ
Cincinnati–Hamilton,	Pittsburgh, PA
OH–KY–IN	Portland–Salem, OR–WA
Denver–Boulder–Greeley, CO	St. Louis, MO–IL
Honolulu, HI	San Diego, CA
Kansas City, MO–KS	Tampa–St. Petersburg–
Milwaukee–Racine, WI	Clearwater, FL
Minneapolis–St. Paul, MN–WI	

What area CPI should I use if there is no CPI for the area in which I live?　17

Although BLS can provide some guidance on this question, users must make the final decision.

As noted in the answers to Questions 14 and 16, BLS strongly urges the use of the national or regional CPIs in escalator clauses. These indexes are more stable and subject to less sampling and other measurement error than are local area indexes and, therefore, more statistically reliable.

Can the CPIs for individual areas be used to compare living costs among areas?　18

No, an individual area index measures how much prices have changed over a specific period in that particular area: it does not show whether prices or living costs are higher or lower in that area relative to another. In general, the composition of the market basket and relative prices of goods and services in the market basket during the expenditure base period vary substantially across areas.

The following illustration shows that, although Area B has higher prices than Area A, the price change in Area A has been greater than in Area B:

| | Base Period | | Current Period | |
	Price	Index	Price	Index
Area A	$0.30	100	$0.55	183
Area B	0.60	100	0.90	150

What types of data are published? 19

Many types of data are published as outputs from the CPI program. The most popular are indexes and percent changes. Requested less often are relative importance (or relative expenditure weight) data, base conversion factors (to convert from one CPI reference period to another), seasonal factors (the monthly factors used to convert unadjusted indexes into seasonally adjusted indexes), and average food and energy prices. Index and price change data are available for the U.S. city average (or national average), for various geographic areas (regions and metropolitan areas), for national population-size classes of urban areas, and for cross-classifications of regions and size classes. Indexes for various groupings of items are available for all geographic areas and size classes.

Individual indexes are available for more than 200 items (for example, apples, men's shirts, and airline fares) and more than 120 different combinations of items (for example, fruits and vegetables, food at home, food and beverages, and "All Items") at the national or U.S. city average level. BLS classifies consumer items into eight major groups: Food and beverages, housing, apparel, transportation, medical care, recreation, education and communication, and other goods and services. (Some indexes are available from as far back as 1913.)

Each month, indexes are published along with short-term percent changes, the latest 12-month change, and, at the national item and group level, unadjusted and (where appropriate) seasonally adjusted percent changes (and seasonal factors), together with annualized rates of change. The annualized rates indicate what the rate of change would be for a 12-month period if a price change measured for a shorter period continued for a full 12 months.

The answer to Question 16 provides information about the areas and size classes for which indexes are published. For areas, BLS publishes less detailed groupings of items than it does for the national level. The following table illustrates this point:

Atlanta, GA   *U.S. City Average*

All items   **All items**
  Food and beverages   Food and beverages
    Food   Food
      Food at home   Food at home
        Cereals and bakery products
        Cereals and cereal products
          Flour and prepared flour mixes
          Breakfast cereal
          Rice, pasta, and corn meal
          Rice
        Bakery products
        Bread
          White bread
          Other breads
        Fresh biscuits, rolls, muffins
        Cakes, cupcakes, and cookies
          Fresh cakes and cupcakes
          Cookies
        Other bakery products
          Fresh sweetrolls, coffeecakes, and doughnuts
          Crackers, bread, and cracker products
          Frozen and refrigerated bakery products, pies, tarts, turnovers

Annual average indexes and percent changes for these groupings are published at the national and local levels.

Semiannual average indexes and percent changes for some of these groupings are also published.

Each month, BLS publishes average price data for some food items (for the U.S. and four regions) and for some energy items (for the U.S., four regions, three size classes, 10 cross-classifications of regions and size classes, and 14 metropolitan areas).

What are some limitations of the CPI?

20

The CPI is subject to both limitations in application and limitations in measurement.

Limitations in application

The CPI may not be applicable to all population groups. For example, the CPI-U is designed to measure the experience with price change of the U.S. urban population and thus may not accurately reflect the experience of people living in rural areas. Also, the CPI does not produce official estimates for the rate of inflation experienced by subgroups of the population, such as the elderly or the poor. (BLS does produce and release an experimental index for the elderly population; however, because of the significant limitations of this experimental index, it should be interpreted with caution.)

As noted in the answer to Question 18, the CPI cannot be used to measure differences in price levels or living costs between one place and another; it measures only time-to-time changes in each place. A higher index for one area does not necessarily mean that prices are higher there than in another area with a lower index. It merely means that prices have risen faster since the two areas' common reference period.

The CPI cannot be used as a measure of total change in living costs, because changes in these costs are affected by factors (such as social and environmental changes and changes in income taxes) that are beyond the definitional scope of the index and so are excluded.

Limitations in measurement

Limitations in measurement can be grouped into two basic types, sampling errors and nonsampling errors.

Sampling errors. Because the CPI measures price changes based on a sample of items, the published indexes differ somewhat from what the results would be if actual records of *all* retail purchases by everyone in the index population could be used to compile the index. These estimating or sampling errors are limitations on the precise accuracy of the index, not mistakes in calculating the index. The CPI program has developed measurements of sampling error, which are updated and published annually in the *CPI Detailed Report*. An increased sample size would be expected to increase accuracy, as well as CPI production costs. The CPI sample design allocates the sample in a way that maximizes the accuracy of the index, given the funds available.

Nonsampling errors. These errors occur from a variety of sources. Unlike sampling errors, they can cause persistent bias in measurements of the index. Nonsampling errors are caused by problems of price data collection, logistical lags in conducting surveys, difficulties in defining basic concepts and their operational implementation, and difficulties in handling the problems of quality change. Nonsampling errors can be far more hazardous to the accuracy of a price index than sampling errors. Hence, BLS expends much effort to minimize these errors. Highly trained personnel ensure the comparability of quality of items from period to period (see answer to Question 8), and collection procedures are extensively documented. The CPI program has an ongoing research and evaluation program to identify and implement improvements in the index.

Will the CPI be updated or revised in the future? 21

Yes. The CPI will need revisions, as long as there are significant changes in consumer buying habits or shifts in population distribution or demographics. By developing annual Consumer Expenditure Surveys and

Point-of-Purchase Surveys, the Bureau has the flexibility to monitor changing buying habits in a timely and cost-efficient manner. In addition, the census conducted every 10 years by the Department of Commerce provides information that enables the Bureau to reselect a new geographic sample that accurately reflects the current population distribution and other demographic factors.

As a matter of policy, BLS is continually researching improved statistical methods. Thus, even between major revisions, further improvements to the CPI are made. For example, until recently, the Bureau would continue to price the brand-name version of a prescription drug even after it lost its patent protection if the brand-name drug was still sold in the selected outlet. Starting in January 1995, BLS changed this policy. Now, 6 months after a drug loses its patent protection, a unique item to be priced is reselected from all therapeutically equivalent drugs (including the original) sold in the selected retail outlet. This approach gives generic versions of the drug a chance to be selected as a substitute. BLS waits until 6 months after the patent expires to give the emerging generic drugs time to gain market share, because the chance of selection is proportional to the sales of each version of the drug in the retail outlet. The new procedure provides a better reflection of consumers' experience with prescription drug prices, because many consumers switch to generic versions of drugs as they become available.

How can I get CPI information? 22

Information on the CPI is available from BLS electronically, through subscriptions to publications and, via telephone and fax, through automated recordings. Information specialists are also available in the national and regional offices to provide assistance.

Electronic access to CPI data

BLS on the Internet. Through the Internet, BLS provides free, easy, and continuous access to almost all published CPI data and press releases. The most recent month's CPI is made available immediately at the time of its release. In addition, a database called LABSTAT, containing current and historical data on the CPI, is accessible. Data and press releases from other BLS surveys also are available. This material is accessible via the World Wide Web (WWW)and File Transfer Protocol (FTP), as described next. Send e-mail to *labstat.helpdesk@bls.gov* for help on how to use any of these systems.

World Wide Web. The BLS Web site at **http://www.bls.gov** provides easy access to LABSTAT, as well as links to program-specific homepages. In addition to furnishing data, the CPI homepage at **http://www.bls.gov/cpi/** provides other CPI information, including a brief explanation of methodology, frequently asked questions and answers, a list of contacts for further information, and explanations of how the CPI handles special items, such as medical care and housing. Furthermore, CPI press releases and historical data for metropolitan areas can be accessed by linking to the regional office homepages from the main BLS Web site.

FTP. This tool provides access to CPI LABSTAT data, as well as to documentation and press release files organized in hierarchical directories. Using your Internet browser, type **http://www.bls.gov**. Next, click on "Get Detailed Statistics" (which is in the horizontal banner near the top of the page), and scroll down to the Prices and Living Conditions section. Then, click on the appropriate "BLS-FTP" button to access the FTP flat files.

Subscriptions to CPI publications

E-mail Subscription Service. The latest U.S. average and local Consumer Price Indexes can be delivered directly to a subscriber's e-mail address on the morning of their release. Just subscribe to one of the nine national and regional CPI subscriptions offered on the BLS News Service (**http://www.bls.gov/bls/list.htm**).

Summary data. Monthly two-page publications containing 1- and 12-month percent changes for selected U.S. city average Consumer Price Index for All Urban Consumers (CPI-U) and the Consumer Price Index for Urban Wage Earners and Clerical Workers (CPI-W) index series. The All Items index data for each local area are also included. To be added to the mailing list, write to Office of Publications, Bureau of Labor Statistics, 2 Massachusetts Avenue, N.E., Room 2850, Washington, DC 20212-0001, or call (202) 691-5200 or any of the BLS regional offices listed toward the end of this document.

CPI Detailed Report. The most comprehensive report of the Consumer Price Index, this publication may be ordered by writing to New Orders, Superintendent of Documents, P.O. Box 371954, Pittsburgh, PA, 15250-7954, or by calling (202) 512-1800. Subscriptions cost $47 per year.

Monthly Labor Review (MLR). The *MLR* provides selected CPI data in a monthly summary of BLS data and occasional articles and methodological descriptions that are too extensive for inclusion in the *CPI Detailed Report*. The *MLR* costs $49 per year and may be ordered by writing to New Orders, Superintendent of Documents, P.O. Box 371954, Pittsburgh, PA, 15250-7954, or by calling (202) 512-1800. The Internet Web site at **http://www.bls.gov/opub/mlr/mlrhome.htm** has issues of the *MLR* back to 1988.

Recorded CPI data

Summary CPI data are provided 24 hours a day on recorded messages. Detailed information on the CPI is available by calling (202) 691-5200 A touch-tone telephone is recommended, as that device allows the user to select specific indexes from lists of available data.

Recorded summaries of CPI data may be obtained by calling any of the following metropolitan-area CPI hot lines:

Area Hotline Numbers

Anchorage (907) 271-2770	Los Angeles (310) 235-6884
Atlanta (404) 331-3415	Miami (305) 358-2305
Baltimore (410) 962-4898	Milwaukee (414) 276-2579
Boston (617) 565-2325	Minneapolis–St. Paul (612) 725-3580
Chicago (312) 353-1800	New York (212) 337-2400
Cincinnati (513) 684-2349	Philadelphia (215) 656-3948
Cleveland (216) 522-3852	Pittsburgh (412) 644-2900
Dallas (214) 767-6970	Portland (503) 231-2045
Denver (303) 844-1726	St. Louis (314) 539-3581
Detroit (313) 226-7558	San Diego (619) 557-6538
Honolulu (808) 541-2808	San Francisco (415) 975-4350
Houston (713) 718-3753	Seattle (206) 553-0645
Indianapolis (317) 226-7885	Washington, DC (202) 606-6994 (202) 691-5200
Kansas City (816) 426-2481	(410) 962-4898

Summaries typically include data for the U.S. city average, as well as the specified area. Recordings are approximately 3 minutes in length and are available 24 hours a day, 7 days a week.

Other sources of CPI data

Technical information may be obtained during normal working hours, Monday through Friday (Eastern Time), by calling (202) 691-7000 or any of the regional offices.

Fax on Demand. A wide variety of BLS information and data, including CPI, are available from the BLS *Ready Facts* catalog via fax on demand. CPI documents from *Ready Facts* that are available around the clock include the monthly CPI press release; selected national, regional, and metropolitan area historical summaries; and some technical information. The latest CPI information is posted during the morning of the day the index is released. To have the latest *Ready Facts* catalog sent to you, call (202) 691-6325, and then follow the instructions given. Each regional office also has a fax system in place; these systems include all information available from the national catalog, in addition to region-specific information on the CPI. Phone and fax-on-demand numbers for the nine regional offices are as follows:

Office	Fax-on-Demand	Telephone
Washington, DC Bureau of Labor Statistics Office of Prices and Living Conditions 2 Massachusetts Avenue, N.E. Washington, DC 20212-0001	(202) 691-6325	(202) 691-7000
Boston Bureau of Labor Statistics Economic Analysis and Information JFK Federal Bldg., E-310 Boston, MA 02203	(617) 565-9167	(617) 565-2327
Philadelphia Bureau of Labor Statistics Economic Analysis and Information The Curtis Center, Suite 610 East 170 South Independence Mall West Philadelphia, PA 19106-3305	(215) 597-4153	(215) 597-3282
New York Bureau of Labor Statistics Economic Analysis and Information 201 Varick Street, Room 808 New York, NY 10014-4811	(212) 337-2412	(212) 337-2400
Atlanta Bureau of Labor Statistics Economic Analysis and Information 61 Forsyth Street, S.W. Room 7T50 Atlanta, GA 30303	(404) 331-3403	(404) 331-3415

Office	Fax-on-Demand	Telephone
Chicago Bureau of Labor Statistics Economic Analysis and Information 230 S. Dearborn Street, Room 960 Chicago, IL 60604	(312) 353-1880	(312) 353-1880
Kansas City Bureau of Labor Statistics Economic Analysis and Information 1100 Main Street, Suite 600 Kansas City, MO 64105-2112	(816) 426-3125	(816) 426-2481
Dallas Bureau of Labor Statistics Economic Analysis and Information 525 Griffin Street, Room 221 Dallas, TX 75202	(214) 767-9613	(214) 767-6970
San Francisco Bureau of Labor Statistics Economic Analysis and Information P.O. Box 193766 San Francisco, CA 94119-3766	(415) 975-4567	(415) 975-4350

QUESTIONS & ANSWERS

Historical tables. These include all published indexes for each of the detailed CPI components. They
may be obtained via the Internet, by calling (202)
691-7000 in the national office, or by contacting any
of the regional offices.

Descriptive publications. These publications de-
scribe the CPI and ways to use it. They include (1)
simple fact sheets discussing specific topics about
the CPI, (2) this pamphlet with its broad, nontechni-
cal overview of the CPI in a question-and-answer
format, and (3) a quite technical and thorough de-
scription of the CPI and its methodology. These publications are available upon request by calling (202)
691-7000, and many are included on the CPI
homepage on the Internet.

Special publications. Also available are various special publications, such as *Relative Importance of
Components in the Consumer Price Index,* and ma-
terials describing the annual revisions of seasonally
adjusted CPI data. For more information, call (202)
691-7000.

Further information may be obtained from the Office of Prices and Living Conditions, Bureau of Labor Statistics, 2 Massachusetts Avenue, N.E., Room
3615, Washington, DC, 20212-0001, telephone (202)
691-7000, or by calling any of the regional offices.

www.ingramcontent.com/pod-product-compliance
Lightning Source LLC
Chambersburg PA
CBHW070755180526
45168CB00004B/1617